About this book

The world is full of different styles of dance, and ballet is one of the most well-known. This book is full of fascinating facts which introduce you to famous dancers and ballet stories you are sure to enjoy.

The theatre is an exciting place before a show. You can see how many people work together to put on a ballet and the stunning costumes and make-up dancers wear.

Find out how to become a ballet dancer and about the other types of dance you can learn. See what a dance studio might look like and the clothes you should wear for your dance lesson.

Look at traditional costumes from around the world and see how national dance differs from country to country.

There are many dance forms for you to explore and the facts are here to help you enjoy the world of dance.

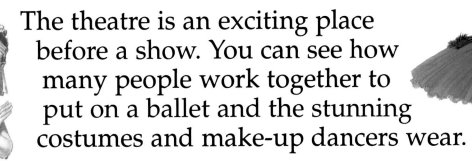

The history of ballet

The tradition of dance dates back thousands of years. People danced to worship their gods, to bring good fortune and to celebrate festivals.

The true origins of ballet, however, date back to Italy, 500 years ago.

Today, ballet is full of variety because of its rich history. Film and television have made it more popular than ever.

During a period in history known as the **Renaissance**, wealthy Italian families entertained visitors at exciting parties with poetry, music, mime and dancing.

Catherine de Médici, an Italian courtier, became Queen of France in 1547. She introduced spectacular dance pageants. They were known as *ballet de cour* as they were danced by the courtiers themselves.

King Louis XIV of France was an enthusiastic dancer. In 1661, he set up a school for dance where the five basic ballet positions were first written down.

Louis XIV as the Sun in the *Ballet de La Nuit*.

4

PUFFIN FACTFINDERS

BALLET
AND DANCE

Written by
Maggie Tucker

Consultant
Amanda Hammond

Edited by
Helen Burnford

PUFFIN BOOKS

The author, Maggie Tucker, trained as a dancer at The Laban Centre for Movement and Dance. She has a BA (Hons) in Dance Theatre and works as a freelance Arts Publicist, promoting Dance, Theatre, Music and children's productions.

The consultant, Amanda Hammond, studied Dance in London, England and Florida, USA. She now teaches contemporary dance.

PUFFIN BOOKS

Published by the Penguin Group
Penguin Books Ltd, 27 Wrights Lane, London W8 5TZ, England
Penguin Books USA Inc., 375 Hudson Street, New York, New York 10014, USA
Penguin Books Australia Ltd, Ringwood, Victoria, Australia
Penguin Books Canada Ltd, 10 Alcorn Avenue, Toronto, Ontario, Canada M4V 3B2
Penguin Books (NZ) Ltd, 182-190 Wairau Road, Auckland 10, New Zealand

Penguin Books Ltd, Registered Offices: Harmondsworth, Middlesex, England

First published 1995
10 9 8 7 6 5 4 3 2 1

Produced for Puffin Books by Zigzag Publishing Ltd, The Barn, Randolph's Farm, Brighton Road, Hurstpierpoint, West Sussex BN6 9EL, England

Series concept: Tony Potter
Managing Editor: Nicola Wright
Production: Zoë Fawcett, Simon Eaton
Designed by Kate Buxton
Illustrated by Peter Dennis/Linda Rogers Associates, Mike Lacy/Simon Girling Associates, Julia Pearson/ Specs Art, Paul Sullivan/David Lewis Illustration
Cover illustration: Stuart McKay and Peter Dennis

Colour separations: Sussex Repro England
Printed by Proost, Belgium

792.8

0140 376 194 4309

Contents

In 1760, **Jean Georges Noverre** introduced story ballets or *ballet d'action*. An early story ballet was *La Fille Mal Gardée* which is still danced today.

A French dancer, called **Marius Petipa**, joined **The Imperial Ballet** in Russia in 1847. He created famous ballets, such as *The Sleeping Beauty*.

In 1909, **Serge Diaghilev** formed **Les Ballets Russes** with the most talented dancers he could find. Diaghilev brought audiences ballets such as *The Firebird* and *Rite of Spring*.

Modern dance began in America with **Isadora Duncan**. She danced barefoot in flowing tunics inspired by Ancient Greece.

Martha Graham in *Night Journey*.

In the 1930s, a new dance technique, with awkward, angular movements, was developed by **Martha Graham**.

5

Ballets old and new entertain audiences with stories of love, magic and far away places.

Some ballets are long, with three or four acts, while others last for just one act.

Not all contemporary ballet and dance tells a story. Sometimes just music and movement alone are fun to watch.

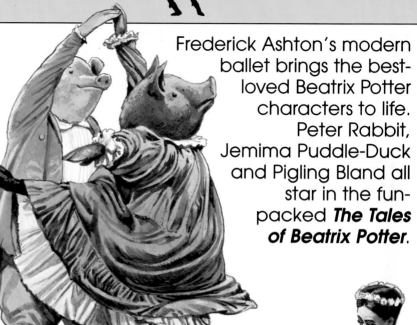

Frederick Ashton's modern ballet brings the best-loved Beatrix Potter characters to life. Peter Rabbit, Jemima Puddle-Duck and Pigling Bland all star in the fun-packed *The Tales of Beatrix Potter*.

In the romantic ballet *La Sylphide*, James falls in love with a forest sprite (a *sylphide*) on the eve of his wedding. He is tricked by a witch and kills the sprite by accident.

The Nutcracker story is set at a Christmas Party. Little Clara dreams that she and her toys are attacked by a mouse king. She defeats him and her favourite toy, the Nutcracker, becomes a handsome prince.

Appalachian Spring is a famous ballet choreographed by Martha Graham. It tells the story of a newly married pioneering couple starting their life on the prairies of America.

Set in a crowded fairground, Fokine's **Petrushka** captures all the excitement of the fair. A magician makes three dolls dance and, when night falls, they secretly come to life on their own.

In **Coppélia**, Dr Coppelius, a toymaker, is tricked into believing that his beautiful doll has come to life!

Unforgettable dancers

Ballet moved to the theatre from the royal palaces over 200 years ago. Ballerinas and male dancers have been popular ever since.

While many dancers are famous for their incredible technique, others have brought something new and exciting to the world of dance.

Taglioni was perfect in the role of the forest sprite in *La Sylphide*.

In the 1830s, **Marie Taglioni** was the first great ballerina. Her lightness and poise brought beauty to every performance. People had never seen such graceful jumps and landings.

One of the most famous male dancers of all time was **Vaslav Nijinsky**. He brought dramatic skill and physical presence to ballet. His amazing leaps and expressive movement gave a special quality to every role he played.

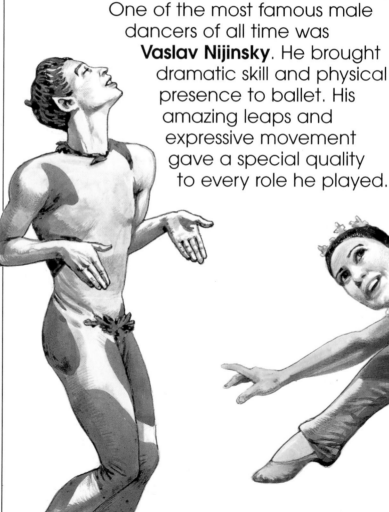

Nijinsky caused a sensation in *L'Après-midi d'un Faune*.

Anna Pavlova was one of the world's greatest dancers. She devoted her whole life to dance. Every role she played seemed magical. She could transform herself into many graceful images.

Pavlova as *The Dying Swan*.

Isadora Duncan is famous for beginning the modern dance movement. She danced freely, wearing a simple tunic.

After defecting from Russia in 1961, **Rudolf Nureyev** danced with the Royal Ballet. He was an exciting, dynamic and strong performer. Male dancing became very popular because of him.

Isadora's movements were inspired by nature.

The choreographer Kenneth MacMillan created *The Prince of the Pagodas* specially for Darcey Bussell.

Margot Fonteyn was a leading ballerina of this century. Her partnership with Rudolph Nureyev was very famous.

Trained at the Royal Ballet School, **Darcey Bussell** is one of today's leading ballerinas.

Ballet is performed and enjoyed throughout the world.

The **Royal Danish Ballet Company** is the world's oldest ballet company. Founded by **August Bournonville**, this company is famous for its powerful male roles and enchanting female stars.

Each country and culture brings something different and new to ballet.

The Australian Ballet is internationally renowned for performances of classical and modern ballets.

From the English Classical style to Cunningham's technique, there is a rich variety of work that celebrates people's love of dance.

Edward Borovansky from the famous Ballet Russes started the Borovansky Ballet in 1939. When he died the company was renamed **The Australian Ballet**.

Arthur Mitchell formed the first black classical ballet company in the US, in 1971. It is called **The Dance Theatre of Harlem**.

The Royal Ballet was originally called the Vic-Wells Ballet. It is now one of the great British ballet companies.

The **Merce Cunningham Dance Company** from the US, is at the forefront of modern dance. Many of the dancers are classically trained.

Merce Cunningham mixes ballet steps with everyday movements.

One of the largest and best known companies is the **Bolshoi Ballet** from Russia. Its colourful and dramatic story ballets are seen all over the world.

You can start dancing from the age of three. In your first lesson you will learn basic steps and exercises.

Stepping, jumping, walking and running will all help to strengthen your muscles, give you better coordination and help you dance in time to the music.

Dance classes are held at local dance schools in the evenings and at weekends. If you want to be a professional dancer you can join a dance academy when you are about eleven years old, or later at sixteen or eighteen years old.

Clothes for dance classes must be light and simple to allow you to move easily.

Boys dance in leotards or T-shirts and tights.

Girls usually wear leotards and tights.

For other dance forms, bare feet, jazz shoes and tap shoes are used.

In a **dance studio** there are usually mirrors on the walls so that you can see that you are moving correctly. The floor is made of wood or vinyl and can be sprung to help you jump.

Ballet shoes are soft and flat, and made from satin, canvas or leather.

The **barre** is a wooden rail attached to the wall which is used to give the dancer support while exercising.

All dance classes are accompanied by **music**. As a dancer you learn to feel and express the music in the way you move.

To become a strong, expressive dancer you must **practise**. Even the most famous dancers go to class every day to stay strong and supple.

When you have learnt the basic ballet steps and can put them together, you are ready to start taking **ballet exams**. Exams test how much you know and show that you are ready to learn more.

The first ballet school was founded by King Louis XIV of France. It was here, in Paris, that the first ballet steps were set and written down. Ever since, the language of ballet has been French.

In a ballet class, you learn each position, or exercise, by its French name.

Before making any shape or position you must have the correct **posture**. This means standing tall with your hips directly over your feet. The back must be straight to give the body a slim line.

En seconde
Second position

En première
First position

En troisième
Third position

It is important to keep the neck relaxed, the head poised and the shoulders open and low.

The first exercise in any ballet class is the *plié*, which means 'to bend'. *Pliés* give the legs strength and suppleness.

Turn out is the amount you can turn your feet sideways in any position. Your legs must be turned outwards from the hip.

The way you carry your arms is called **ports de bras**. Arms should make a gentle curve and move gracefully.

Fingers should always be slightly curved and soft.

En quatrième
Fourth position

En cinquième
Fifth position

There are **five basic positions** for the feet and arms. They are used at the beginning and end of movements and in passing from one movement to another.

The order of exercises in a ballet class has been developed over hundreds of years. Each class starts at the **barre**.

After exercising at the *barre*, dancers move to the centre of the room for **centre practice**. Here the *barre* exercises are practised without support.

Pointing the toes correctly is an important part of ballet. Your foot should be pointed from the ankle with the leg turned out. This way your foot should make a straight line with your leg.

To become a professional dancer takes a great deal of dedication and hard work.

There are many complicated movements to learn and master.

Ballerinas and leading male dancers have studied, practised and performed for many years before gaining world fame.

Girls start to learn **pointework** at about age eleven. This means dancing on the tips of their toes, wearing special **pointe shoes**.

The toe of a **pointe shoe** is hardened with layers of satin, paper and coarse material called **burlap**.

A series of exercise positions and movements, performed together, is called an **enchaînement**.

Many dancers join a ballet company as a member of the **corps de ballet** or chorus. Performing as a group of dancers they learn to work together and to play a character on stage.

You can start training to become a professional ballet dancer aged sixteen. This takes at least two years, working and dancing for many hours a day.

The **arabesque** is one of the most beautiful ballet positions. It requires perfect balance while standing on one leg, with the other stretched out behind.

As dancers complete their training, they start to look for jobs. To become a member of a **dance company** they must **audition**. This means taking part in a class and performing a solo in front of a panel of experts.

A **pirouette** is an exciting and difficult step where the dancer spins on one leg. This needs balance and strength.

The **pas de deux** is a partnership between two dancers. The male dancer lifts and supports his partner.

Modern dance

Ballet is the oldest dance technique in the Western world, but many other dance forms are taught at schools throughout the world. These include contemporary dance, tap and jazz.

Contemporary dance is about a hundred years old. Its founders wanted to make movement more natural and expressive. **Graham**, **Cunningham** and **Humphrey** are names of techniques.

Contemporary dancers usually dance barefoot.

Contemporary dance has different sets of positions to ballet. There may be **floor movements** and dancers can use their breathing to help form the different positions.

These techniques are very different from ballet, but a knowledge of ballet can help when learning them.

Tap dancing was started by African slaves in America. Traditional African dances were mixed with those of white people. Over the years, tap steps have been made into the method which is taught in schools today.

Fred Astaire was one of the most famous tap dancers. He was both a talented dancer and choreographer.
Today, dancers such as **Savion Glover** continue to make tap dancing very popular.

Tap dancing is very fast and rhythmic. In **musicals** there are often as many as thirty dancers all tap dancing at the same time. The sound they make is very exciting.

Tap shoes have metal toe and heel plates fitted to make a special sound on the floor.

Jazz dancing started in America. It developed from a mixture of African and European dances. Like tap dance, it is used in musicals and is also known as **show dancing**.

Dancers who work in musicals are trained in many dance techniques. They are adaptable and perform ballet, tap and jazz.

19

Costumes and make-up

Ballet does not use speech, so dancers must use all their expressive skills to convey their mood and character.

Costumes, make-up and mime are all important for telling a ballet story and setting the scene.

Early ballet dancers started to wear shorter and looser clothes as they began to perform more complicated steps.

Dancing tights were invented by Maillot at the Paris Opera in the early 1800s. They allowed dancers to wear shorter dresses without showing their bare legs!

Early ballet masters created **mime gestures** which have become part of today's choreography. Using movements of the eyes, arms and head, dancers can convey the emotions and intentions of the characters they play.

Some costumes look as if they are very hard to dance in but they are made of very light-weight materials.

Theatre lights are so bright, dancers wear make-up to stop their skin from looking pale and shiny.

A dancer's hair is usually tied back from her face so that her eyes and mouth can be clearly seen.

Hair is often decorated with a **head-dress** or flowers.

Costumes must be strong and easy to move in. They can be made from silk, velvet, chiffon or lycra and decorated with beads, braid and ribbons.

Tutus have short, stiff skirts which stick out from the waist.

The **classical tutu** was designed so that dancers could perform difficult turns, such as *fouèttés*, for which their legs needed to move freely.

Stage make-up is bright and heavy. It has to be applied boldly so that it can be seen from a distance.

Some dances look so natural and spontaneous it seems as though the dancers are making up the steps.

Every dance has been carefully worked out and set to music by the choreographer.

The **choreographer** chooses the story, selects the music and arranges the steps for a ballet. The ideas may come from a fairy tale, a painting or a poem.

Movements from *Square Dance* by Balanchine.

George Balanchine was a famous choreographer who created over a hundred ballets. He made dances which were both graceful and athletic.

Modern choreographers often create abstract dances with no story.

Twyla Tharp is a contemporary choreographer who uses movement of all kinds. Her work includes ballet and jazz dance.

Igor Stravinsky was one of the most distinguished composers to write ballet music. He worked with famous choreographers such as **Fokine** and **Balanchine**.

A scene from Petipa's staging of *Swan Lake.*

Keeping a written record of dance pieces is called **notation** or **choreology**. This means ballets can be accurately recreated. The **Benesh** system is most commonly used to write down movements in classical ballet. **Labanotation** is used to record contemporary dance.

Music is a basic ingredient of nearly all dance. Choreographers sometimes ask a composer to write new music for a ballet. **Marius Petipa** worked with the famous ballet composer, **Pyotr Ilyich Tchaikovsky**. He wrote the magical music for *The Sleeping Beauty, The Nutcracker* and *Swan Lake.*

Benesh notation from *Les Sylphides.*

Everyone in a ballet company has a part to play in putting on a successful show.

The dance is choreographed, or designed, to fit the theatre. The stage is carefully lit and the scenery painted.

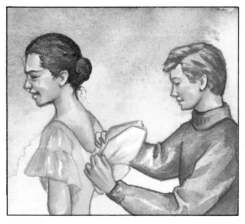

There must be rehearsals and time for costumes to be made or repaired.

Stage hands or **dressers** must check where to stand backstage to help a dancer with a quick costume change.

The **stage manager** and **technical crew** check that all the scenery and props are safe and in place.

The **dress rehearsal**, when costumes are first worn, is the last chance to practise before **opening night**.

A good **lighting designer** can transform the stage and create a magical atmosphere by the way the lights are positioned.

The **designer** and choreographer plan the **scenery** and **costumes**. The designer makes a model to check everything will fit on stage.

A technician organises the **special effects**. A dry-ice machine might be used to blow mist across the stage.

The **publicity officer** lets the public know about the show. Programmes and posters are printed and the stars of the show may appear on television or radio.

Dancers practise with the **orchestra** for the last few rehearsals.

The stage has clear markings so that everyone knows where to stand.

Dancers spend many hours with the **choreographer**, rehearsing for the show. They start by learning the basic steps, then put them to music.

Dance for fun

People all over the world get together to dance for fun and to meet people.

Ceroc is a new and exciting form of modern jive based on French Rock 'n' Roll. There are steps to learn but you can dance to almost any kind of music.

Social dance is affected by fashion and is often inspired by films and music.

Rap, rave and **cult dance** all rely on the beat and sound of the loud music. The DJ plays the music the dancers want to hear!

The Waltz is perhaps one of the most famous social dances. It was first danced in Germany in 1780 when the swinging turns and the close contact between partners were considered shocking!

Johann Strauss wrote the music which made the waltz popular.

Ballroom dancers often take part in competitions.

Ballroom dancing is very popular. **Old-time**, **Modern** and **Latin American** are all types of ballroom dancing.

Latin dance came from South America, with lively dances such as the Rumba, Samba and Mambo.

Latin music is very rhythmic and noisy!

The **Jitterbug** and **Boogie-Woogie** were thrilling new dances in the 1940s. They were brought to Great Britain by American and Canadian soldiers during World War II. These dances are now known as **jive**.

Rock 'n' Roll became popular in the 1950s when records became cheap enough for young people to buy. Dancers jumped, turned and twisted to music by popular singers such as Bill Haley and Elvis Presley.

The Alligator and **The Monkey** were fashionable 1960s dances.

Dances like **The Twist** and **The Mashed Potato** were invented in the 1960s when people began to dance on their own.

Disco dancing began in the 1970s. You do not have to dance in pairs and there are no set steps. The way you look and move are more important.

27

Every country has its own dance form. National dances grow from religion, folk tales and even the weather.

Colourful costumes and decorations are part of each country's national dance.

India has a tremendous diversity of peoples, climates, languages and dances. One of the most popular is **Bharata Natyam** which started as part of religious worship, 2,000 years ago. A story is told using hand movements and facial expressions.

The dancer's bare feet tap out complex rhythmic patterns.

In England, **Morris dancing** is traditionally danced by men. They wear bells and ribbons and dance in lines facing each other. A man called the 'fool' carries a colourful stick and hits anyone who misses a step!

The Polish **Mazurka** is danced by eight or sixteen couples in a circle.

The main Spanish dancing styles are regional dances like the **fandango** and **flamenco**. Flamenco has developed from Asian, Arabic and gypsy dancing.

Settlers in the USA have created many country dances. At a **Square Dance** the 'caller' tells the dancers what to do. Dancers swing their partners as the banjo and fiddle play.

In **Irish dancing**, the upper body is kept straight and stiff while the legs and feet kick and step.

Irish dancers' costumes are embroidered with Celtic designs.

Flamenco is often danced to the music of guitars and castanets.

The **Maoris** of New Zealand use dance to communicate. As they dance they chant, quiver their hands and use facial expressions. The dancing is often accompanied by a sung poem.

The **Scottish Reel** is a gliding and springing dance performed by couples. Music is played on the bagpipes. The men wear a pleated, tartan kilt which is like a skirt.

Women wear a white dress with a tartan sash for dancing.

Ballet school life

Anyone who wants to become a professional ballet dancer will need to train hard for many years.

Ballet schools give every student the chance to dance the best they can, to discover their talents and, perhaps, become a famous dancer.

To win a place at ballet school, you must attend an audition and an interview. The **audition** is a simple class where examiners look at your height, the shape of your feet and your personality. They also look for musicality – the way you dance with the music.

Ballet schools are much like any other schools. Pupils study for exams and learn the usual subjects, such as English, Maths and Biology. They also have special lessons including Music, Drama, History of Dance, Singing and Contemporary Dance.

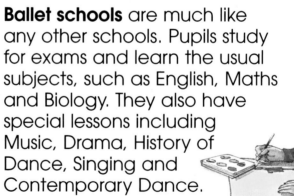

When pupils reach the age of sixteen, they begin to learn **ballet repertory** and **classical pas de deux**.

Once a year, pupils at **The Royal Ballet School** put on a performance at Covent Garden Opera House in London.

Being involved in a performance is excellent practice for the future. Not only do dancers learn about the art of performing but also the demands of **rehearsals** and the many jobs involved in producing a show.

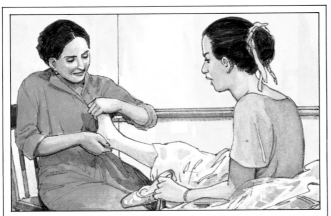

A thorough training in dance opens up many career opportunities. Dancers can become choreographers, stage managers, administrators, teachers and **physiotherapists**.

Days are long and demanding but dancers must have a good all-round education as not every student will take up a career as a dancer.

A career as a dancer is not easy or secure. Not everyone will grow to the right height and there is always the risk of injury. Dancing is not just a career - it is a way of life which can be very exciting and rewarding.

Index